Classic Instruction

The American
Golfer

The American Golfer titles may be purchased for business or promotional use or for special sales. For information, please write to: The American Golfer, Inc., 200 Railroad Avenue, Greenwich, Connecticut 06830.

THE AMERICAN GOLFER and its logo, its name in scripted letters, are trademarks of The American Golfer, Inc.

Photographs of Ben Crenshaw by Steve Szurlej.
Photograph on doublegate opener by ALLSPORT.

SECOND EDITION

ISBN 1-888531-10-61

ESN 9781888531060

Published by:
The American Golfer, Inc.
200 Railroad Avenue
Greenwich, Connecticut 06830
(203) 862-9720
FAX (203) 862-9724
imd@aol.com
www.theamericangolfer.com

"To me, his style of writing was as elegant as his own swing, and will always be an important part of golf's literature."

—**BEN CRENSHAW**
from *The Greatest of Them All:*
The Legend of Bobby Jones:

Classic Instruction

by Bobby Jones and Ben Crenshaw

Edited by Martin Davis

THE AMERICAN GOLFER

200 Railroad Avenue • Greenwich, Connecticut 06830

203-862-9720 • imd@aol.com

Contents

Classic Instruction

by Martin Davis

While I was researching my earlier biography on Jones, *Bobby Jones: The Greatest of Them All*, I was given access to Bob's files and memorabilia at Alston & Bird, the law firm in Atlanta that Bob helped establish. In a conference room, aptly named after him and featuring the original architect's rendering of the Augusta National Golf Course, were assembled approximately 20 boxes of assorted records and photographs for my review. Many of the pictures in these boxes chronicled Bob's life and had never been published. The Jones family kindly gave me permission to use these in my biography of Bob.

As I pored through these boxes, I came across a small black box containing approximately 100 instructional photos of Bob Jones with numbers on the back keyed to a series of handwritten yellow legal pages covering each aspect of the game—the grip, woods, long irons, short irons, sand play, putting and chipping. Looking through the box, my eyes widened. It was as if I had discovered the Rosetta Stone for golfers—the keys to the game handwritten by the master himself!

Among true golf afficionados, I doubt there would be much debate with the notion that golf's popularity today is attributable, in large part, to what Bob Jones accomplished. Think, for a moment, about what he did.

Bob's record as a competitor is unparalleled: he won thirteen national championships in an eight-year span, with four of these coming in the Grand Slam year of 1930. A lifelong amateur, Jones accomplished a feat no one has been able to duplicate to this very day — winning all four of the era's major championships in one year. When Jones played against the leading professionals, the press referred to it as "Jones against the field." He was that good.

Bob also established a standard for golf as a game of personal honor and individual responsibility. He twice called penalties on himself in competition, in all likelihood costing him two additional national championships. When asked about it, he replied, "you might as well praise a man for not robbing a bank," his innate sense of modesty and decency shining through.

Bob founded the Augusta National Golf Club, was instrumental in the design of the course and began the Masters, the pinnacle of golf tournaments.

But beyond these grand accomplishments, he left us with much more. Bob Jones's ability to communicate—whether via the wonderful short Warner Brothers films he wrote and starred in or through his books and magazine articles—was as important as his exploits on the course. He gave us a sense of what the game was all about and how to play it.

Upon investigation, I learned that the materials I unearthed in that long forgotten little black box were used in a limited series of film strips sold in the mid 1930s. Incredibly, the manuscript and pictures had never been published. Needless to say, I asked permission to publish this treasure. To my great joy, Ben Crenshaw, an admirer of Bob Jones and a serious student of the game and its history, agreed to coauthor the book. To best illustrate Ben's commentary, Steve Szurlej, one of golf's finest instructional photographers, photographed Ben's swing, at approximately the same position and angle as was shown in the photos taken of Jones in 1933.

Interestingly, Ben had never met Bob Jones—Ben's first appearance at the Masters came shortly after Bob had passed away. However, given Ben's strong connection with Augusta and his feelings about Bob Jones's role in golf as well as the classic nature of Ben's golf swing, there can be no argument that there is a direct historical linkage between the two.

To place this in perspective, we asked Byron Nelson, who knew both Bob Jones and Ben Crenshaw quite well, to write a forward, which he finished shortly before his passing this past fall. I hope you enjoy this new edition.

INTRODUCTION

Classic Instruction

by Ben Crenshaw

To my way of thinking, Bob Jones was a true Renaissance man. He not only played the game of golf at its very highest level, but wrote about it as well as anyone ever has. Bob's instruction book, *Golf Is My Game*, along with Harvey Penick's insightful lessons, provided the basis for my learning the game.

As golfers, we are truly blessed with the wonderful body of literature that has developed around the game. No other sport I know boasts the high calibre of writers that golf has consistently produced through the years: Bernard Darwin, Herbert Warren Wind, Henry Longhurst, Pat Ward-Thomas, Grantland Rice, Dan Jenkins, Peter Dobreiner and Charlie Price, to name a few.

Bob Jones, perhaps the greatest of golf's champions, certainly belongs in this exalted company of fine writers. His books, *Down the Fairway*, *Golf Is My Game* and *Bobby Jones on Golf*, as well as his articles appearing in *The American Golfer* magazine, have had great impact on people's enjoyment and understanding of the game. Bob's unique ability to clearly and concisely convey his thoughts on the game in general, and on the swing in particular, is one of golf's greatest treasures.

The photographs and accompanying copy that Martin Davis unearthed in researching our earlier book on Jones were an unbelievable find. Given the quality of these materials, we have chosen to use Bob Jones's exact words as he wrote them in longhand in 1933, along with the very photos he selected to illustrate each element of the golf swing.

Virtually all of what Bob Jones wrote about in these pages is applicable today. As a supplement to what Bob wrote, I have attempted to emphasize certain points he is making and also to point out the differences in the way I approach the game.

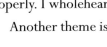

Several recurrent themes throughout the book are worth mentioning.

First and foremost, Bob emphasized the importance of a proper grip. He felt a sound grip was the foundation for playing the game properly. I wholeheartedly agree.

Another theme is the narrow stance Bob

used throughout *all* of his shots. To illustrate this, we have superimposed on the photos of both Bob and myself at the address position with various clubs white guidelines indicating the width of our relative stances. In comparison with the way I stand to the ball, you will notice just how narrow Bob's address position was with all of his clubs, including the putter. Bob felt the narrow stance encouraged a proper turn back and through the ball.

This narrow stance provided him with the base to truly *swing* the club, another recurrent theme in the book. No other great golfer stood with such a narrow stance as Bob Jones.

As you can well imagine, because of the improvements in the implements we play with today and the strides made in course conditioning, the nature of the golf swing has changed somewhat from Bob Jones's day. Although Bob's swing was more of a "hands swing"— to compensate for the inherent torque of the hickory shafts, the basic fundamentals of proper form remain unchanged. It seems altogether fitting to hold this classic golf swing as a model for today's golfers.

As is widely known, Bob Jones had a very inventive and active mind.

He learned the game as a boy by copying his Scottish pro, Stuart Maiden, and experimenting with different techniques that seemed to work best for him. Luckily for us, these techniques also work well for most golfers

and continue to do so to this very day.

Today, it seems, the emphasis in the game is on power and hitting the ball high. It's a more violent game. To my way of thinking, Bob Jones's golf swing was far more elegant than many we see today. It was one of the most lyrical and rhythmical swings ever. It's just as Bernard Darwin said, "…there was a touch of poetry to it."

I urge you to try some of the techniques Bob and I describe on the following pages. I think it they will improve your game. At the very least, they should enhance your understanding of what goes into a good golf swing.

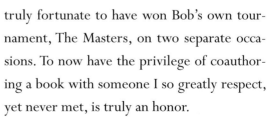

I have been truly fortunate to have won Bob's own tournament, The Masters, on two separate occasions. To now have the privilege of coauthoring a book with someone I so greatly respect, yet never met, is truly an honor.

I hope you enjoy the fruits of our labor— even though they occurred many, many years apart.

Two Great Friends

by Byron Nelson

It was my great honor to meet Bob Jones when I played in my first Masters Tournament in 1935, the second Masters ever played. He was very cordial and congratulated me for qualifying for the tournament. He said he was glad that I was there and hoped that I would become a good player. That meant a lot to me coming from the man who had won the Grand Slam just a few years before.

Jones had the greatest name in golf in his time, of course, and is still considered great today. He was a wonderful man, with great knowledge about the history of the game and the best way to play. His ability to judge players and know what they needed to do to play good golf was excellent. Very educated and quite articulate, Jones wrote many articles and several books on golf.

I'll never forget that '35 Masters Tournament, not only because it was my first Masters, but because as I was coming up the 17th fairway, I stopped to watch Gene Sarazen hit his second shot from the adjoining fairway to the par-5 15th green. Of course, that shot found the cup for a double eagle two, and turned out to be one of the most famous shots in the whole history of golf.

After I won my first Masters in 1937, I got to know Bob well. As the winner, I got to see more of him and would occasionally come to Augusta to play golf with him. I played a lot of golf with Bob over the next few years and wound up close to him. I fondly recall a match I played there with Bob Jones against Henry Picard and Gene Sarazen. We were all playing well that day, including Bob, and on the back nine, Henry and Gene made seven straight birdies — but never won a hole from us. Jones shot 31 on the back nine that day. Amazing.

Byron Nelson and Bob Jones at The Masters in the late 1930's.

In the early years of The Masters it was a tradition for Bob to play in the last group of the fourth round with the third round leader. However, when Bob became sick with that debilitating disease of the spinal column in the late 1940's and couldn't play any longer, Bob asked me to take over his ceremonial role of playing with the third round leader in Sunday's final round. It was certainly one of the nicest honors I ever received. Since I had retired from active competition in 1946 and Bob had personally asked me to be his stand-in, I enthusiastically accepted. It was a great honor from one of the greatest players of all time and one of the finest individuals I have ever known. (I represented Bob in the last group at The Masters until the 1956 tournament. As you may recall, Ken Venturi — an amateur at the time — was the third round leader. The competition committee met before the fourth round and decided that it would be unfair for me to play with Ken as it would have given him an unfair advantage to play the final round with his golf instructor.)

Bob's golf swing was quite elegant — it was a long swing with great rhythm and it had wonderful pace. I think he learned that wonderful swing by originally playing with hickory clubs — he sure had to wait on the action of the hickory to square up the clubface at impact. He was longer at the top of his back swing than modern players and he had a lot of action with his feet and legs, almost like a dancer. His whole motion was free and easy with all of his strokes, including his putting. And his touch around the greens was excellent. In comparison with the modern game, his stance for all of his shots was narrower than players today. He turned more than is the custom today and that is where he got his freedom.

On the greens, several things made him great — Bob's putting stroke just flowed through. It was smooth and fairly long and there was no hit at the ball. If you look at the comparison putting photos of Bob and Ben Crenshaw on pages 45-49, you'll see an uncanny resemblance between the two. Having played golf with both of them, although many years apart, their putting strokes were quite similar — both with just gorgeous motion in their putting strokes — great rhythm, similar erect positions and no "hit" at the ball. These are great things for a player of any era to keep in mind.

On a personal note you might say Ben Crenshaw is the modern day successor to all of those wonderful attributes that Bob Jones embodied — sterling character, a reverence for the game and its traditions and the ability to write and communicate well. And you might also say Ben's golf swing is the logical development of the classic golf swing that began with Bob Jones and developed through the years. Both had swings of great beauty, although achieved with far different equipment many years apart.

Although they never met, Bob would have greatly admired and appreciated Ben. It certainly has been my pleasure to know, play golf and be associated with these two fine gentlemen.

The photos in this book bring back a lot of memories of Bob's swing — and Ben's too. Bob's concise written instruction is just how I remember the way he talked and explained things.

I think you will enjoy this book from two great friends.

— Byron Nelson,
August 2006

Byron and Ben Crenshaw
in the early 1990's.

■ *The Grip*

CRENSHAW:

Bob Jones believed that the foundation for a good golf swing was a fundamentally sound grip which enabled the left arm to play a dominant role in guiding the swing.

The grip I use does not differ much at all from Bob's grip.

JONES:

The first, and perhaps most important step towards learning golf is to acquire a correct grip. The hands must be placed upon the club in proper relation to each other, the face of the club and to other parts of the player's body.

The left hand must be placed in a position of power, to some extent on the top of the shaft. As I grip the club, I can see three knuckles of this hand as I look down upon it.

CRENSHAW:

In order to make full use of the left arm, Jones employed a "strong" grip—he placed the left hand well over the shaft so that the left thumb was on the right side of the shaft and the first three knuckles of the left hand faced the golfer.

A few people these days advocate a little weaker grip in the left hand, but Jones' grip is still fundamentally sound. For example, Ben Hogan wanted his thumb on top of the shaft whereas Byron Nelson, Sam Snead and Jones definitely preferred a stronger grip.

As kids, Harvey Penick encouraged us to "...show him some left hand"—meaning using a strong grip as Bob Jones is doing here. It is a very powerful position.

■ The Grip

JONES:

The right hand approaches the shaft in this way, with palm to the front, and grips the shaft in the fingers.

CRENSHAW:

It is important to note the way Bob is going to place his right hand on the club—with the web of his right hand and grasping the grip in the base of his fingers.

CRENSHAW:

Harvey Penick taught me to grip the club in a similar way. He said grip the club like you would a yardstick.

Start with the web of your right hand to the side of the shaft and place the bottom of the shaft at the base of your fingers. Then simply wrap your fingers around it.

Harvey put it another way, "...simply shake hands with the club."

■ *The Grip*

CRENSHAW:

CRENSHAW:

This is an excellent
view showing
the index finger
separated from the
other three fingers
of the right hand.
The thumb and the
forefinger of the right
hand provide feel and
balance throughout
the swing.

In terms of grip
pressure, nothing
much has changed
today. Bob wanted to
grip a little more
firmly with his left
hand and a little
more sensitively
with his right so that
he could exercise
control throughout
the swing with his
dominant left arm.

Proper grip
pressure has the
effect of unlocking
the wrists.

JONES:

The grip must be positive, but never tense.
The firmest pressure is exerted by the three
smaller fingers (those visible here) of the
left hand. The grip of the right hand is very
light.

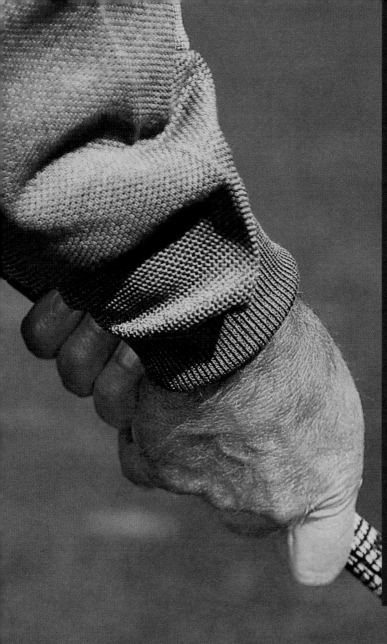

CRENSHAW:

I've always felt that if you grip the club too tightly, you won't be able to feel the clubhead.

I like to grip the club lightly enough so as to make the clubhead feel heavy when I swing. A smooth, rhythmical swing is not possible without feeling the clubhead.

Obviously, the converse is true: the tighter you grip it, the lighter the clubhead will feel, thereby lessening your ability to make a smooth swing.

Given today's equipment and the emphasis on power, we tend to grip the club a little tighter than in Bob Jones's day. However, sensitively gripping the club is still paramount.

JONES:

The little finger of the right hand aids compactness by overlapping the index finger of the left, but...

CRENSHAW:

It is interesting to note that Bob let his right little finger rest in the groove formed between the index and second finger of his left hand. While there are many variations of the basic grip, some better players put the little finger of the right hand on top of the second knuckle of the index finger of the left hand.

Whichever way you grip the club, the most important thing is to position the two hands and fingers so as to achieve a secure grip that works as one piece.

…the fingers twine around the shaft providing an ample spread to make manipulation of the clubhead easy.

CRENSHAW:

Once again, proper grip pressure cannot be overemphasized in allowing the clubhead to swing.

To me, this photograph of Bob epitomizes proper grip pressure— it appears sensitive, ready and responsive. There is not a hint of tightness whatsoever.

27

■ Woods

JONES:

The first position should be comfortable. The feet are separated by approximately the width of the shoulders and both toes are turned slightly outward.

CRENSHAW:

I don't see how anyone could be more relaxed or better balanced over the golf ball. It's just the most beautiful position!

In viewing Bob's address position— a relatively narrow stance with his feet shoulder-width apart—remember that Jones was trying to put the club in motion by making full use of his hips and legs to achieve a full swing.

Bob always felt that the proper ball position with the driver was off the left instep so that there would not be any weight shift necessary to provide a sweeping motion through impact.

CRENSHAW:

As you can see, I tend to stand a little wider than Bob. Today most people are taught to restrict their hip turn to 45° while fully turning their shoulders to 90°. To do so you should employ a wider stance.

Both approaches are valid. If you want to make full use of your body throughout the swing, use a narrower stance. If a more restrictive swing is desired, then stand a bit wider. Try both and see which makes more sense for you.

■ **Woods**

CRENSHAW:

**Note how his arms
hang down naturally
and how it appears
that he's ready to
move in any
direction. With a
rounded back and
straight legs,
this is an "arms
hanging" method.
Although it's an older
method, it looks so
beautifully relaxed
and comfortable that
no one could go
wrong by copying
this set-up position.**

JONES:

The stance is squared, that is,
with the feet about equal distance
from the line of play.

CRENSHAW:

At address, today's player is taught to have a straighter back with a little more bend in the knees. Quite frankly, I don't know which method is better.

■ Woods

Bob's takeaway definitely stems from the hickory-shafted era. His initial move away from the ball is quite similar to the one used by Byron Nelson—letting the clubhead drag its way back almost before the hips move. The hands move first and the feeling is that the clubhead is almost lagging behind.

Together with a narrow stance, the result is a full pivot and turn. If you feel that your body isn't turning, try this method.

JONES:

The backward movement originated in the center of the body. One has the feeling that the club is being pushed by the left side and left arm.

32

33

■ Woods

CRENSHAW:

**Today's golfer does
not cock his wrists
this early in the
swing. This simply
has to do with the
takeaway itself.**

**Bob made ample
use of his wrists,
hands and arms in
the backswing.**

JONES:

The swing progresses for
some distance before the hands
begin to elevate the club and
the first cocking of the wrists
becomes apparent.

CRENSHAW:

Bob emphasized the importance of a full backswing. If that meant that the club went past parallel, that was perfectly fine.

He wanted a full hip and shoulder turn. He felt that the club was easier to keep in motion if there was a nice full turn.

Note how much his left heel comes off the ground—that's certainly one thing that's different from today.

In this position he is truly coiled.

JONES:

In completing the backward wind-up, the back is turned almost squarely to the hole. The swing is of ample length carrying the club past a horizontal position.

What an absolutely beautiful backswing!

When Bob reached the top, he wanted the clubhead to cross the line and appear to be pointing to the right of his target. He felt that it was much easier to return your arms to your side, thus keeping your hands underneath the swing plane.

By swinging in this manner, you would not come over the top and produce a slice with a pronounced out-to-in swing path.

If you compare this photograph of Bob with the previous one, you'll note his hips are starting to unwind as he plants his left heel.

JONES:

The hips lead as the unwinding begins, and by pulling against the hands and the weight of the club, draw the left arm taut.

JONES:

The cock of the wrists is preserved during the early stages of the downstroke while the head of the club drops behind the player so that it can approach the ball from the inside.

CRENSHAW:

This is an ideal position. Significantly, there is no effort for the club to come out and over the intended line of flight. Putting the club in this position can only be achieved as a result of the proper unwinding of the left side during the early stages of the downswing. It cannot be achieved if the upper body takes over first.

Note carefully the position of the right elbow: it is close to the right side, but not cramped.

Every bit of power in the hips, legs and back goes into the blow, which is directed along the line upon which the ball is intended to travel.

This is absolutely perfect. Note how Bob's left hip and left side are out of the way, making room for the arms to come through. His weight has shifted to the left side with his right toe supporting his right side; his right knee, right hand and right shoulder are all kicking-in to square the blow.

His head is still in back of where the ball was at address, perfectly illustrating the "stay-behind-the-ball" school of thought.

JONES:

The left arm remains perfectly straight and no roll of the right hand over the left takes place until after the ball has been started on its way.

CRENSHAW:

No one can achieve a more perfect position.

If you look at today's great players, you'll see that they all arrive at this same position regardless of how they start their swing. It is a very athletic position. Byron Nelson always said that a good position at impact is with the chin over the right knee.

There couldn't be a better image for golfers to keep in mind when they reach impact.

Note how Bob's left arm is ramrod straight. That's power!

CRENSHAW:

Note how I'm slightly behind the ball at impact, yet exerting the maximum power.

43

CRENSHAW:

Again this is a great position to copy. What's important just past impact is how long Bob stays down and through the ball with his right shoulder coming under his chin. There's absolutely no effort to lift the ball into the air.

JONES:

A brassie shot from the fairway is hit hard and slightly downward in order to cause the ball to rise and pursue a controlled course.

44

■ Long Irons

CRENSHAW:

Note how Bob's feet are narrower than even his somewhat narrow stance with the driver.

The narrowness of the stance allowed Jones to swing the club further around his body. Remember that Jones' Scottish teacher, Stewart Maiden, learned to swing to keep the ball down and out of the wind. They played a "ground" or "running" game in the U.K.

As a result, the swing that Jones learned, especially with the longer clubs, was more around his body with a very full shoulder turn. He wanted a flatter swing that would produce a lower ball flight.

CRENSHAW:

Today's game is more of a power game or an "air" game with the objective to hit the ball high.

The stance at address is wider and the backswing is more upright.

Both approaches are certainly valid.

If you want to use more of your body in your swing, to unlock and activate your lower body, experiment with the width of the stance. You'll find more fluidity from the waist down with a narrower stance.

JONES:

The drag away from
the ball. The clubhead
lags because the
hips and legs start
the movement while
the hands and
wrists are relaxed.

CRENSHAW:

Bob's move away
from the ball is quite
different than the
way it is done today.
In the modern golf
swing, the clubhead
starts to move first.

CRENSHAW:

The backswing stays a little more on line and then it picks up, resulting in a higher hand position at the top of the swing.

JONES:

At this stage there has scarcely been any change in the relation of arms, hands and club,…

CRENSHAW:

■ Notice how as Bob is taking the club back, his left foot is already coming off the ground early in the backswing.

CRENSHAW:

In contrast, my left foot tends to stay on the ground for a longer period of time.

51

JONES:

…but here the hands begin to pick up the movement as the turning of the hips and shoulders continues.

CRENSHAW:

As Jones turns away from the ball, note how he is markedly taking the club to the inside primarily with his hands.

CRENSHAW:

Contrast the photo of Bob on the opposite page with image of this image of a more modern swing on this page. In my swing, the club continues back in a straight-line fashion and then moves up.

JONES:

The right elbow meanwhile keeps close to the side, but it is not cramped against the ribs. The right arm is completely relaxed while the left pushes the club back in a wide arc.

CRENSHAW:

This is an excellent example of how Maiden taught Jones to allow the left arm to guide the swing on the way back. Nothing has really changed to this day.

Although this is as correct for today's player as for those in Jones' day, it is what happens just prior to this sequence that is different from the modern approach.

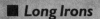

JONES:

The wind-up of the hips is complete at this point. The club is about horizontal and the left arm shows a slight curve.

CRENSHAW:

Although this is a beautiful position at the top of the backswing, a player of today would most likely show less hip wind-up and have the left heel remain on the ground throughout the backswing.

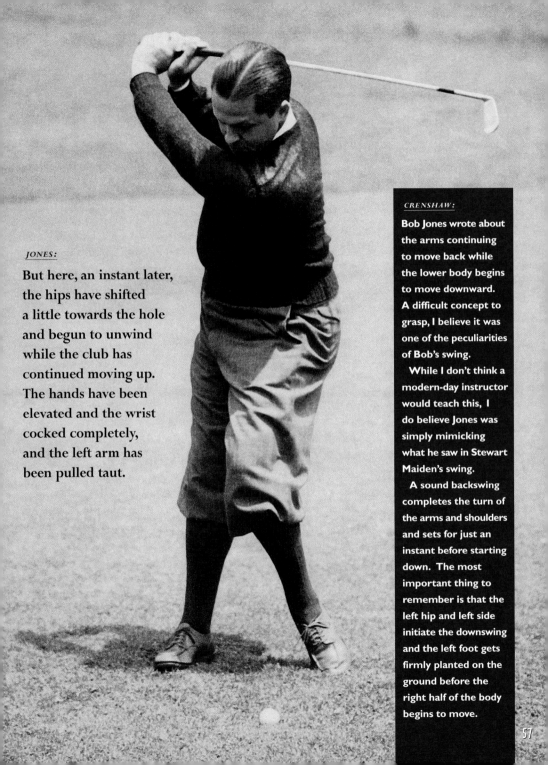

But here, an instant later, the hips have shifted a little towards the hole and begun to unwind while the club has continued moving up. The hands have been elevated and the wrist cocked completely, and the left arm has been pulled taut.

Bob Jones wrote about the arms continuing to move back while the lower body begins to move downward. A difficult concept to grasp, I believe it was one of the peculiarities of Bob's swing.

While I don't think a modern-day instructor would teach this, I do believe Jones was simply mimicking what he saw in Stewart Maiden's swing.

A sound backswing completes the turn of the arms and shoulders and sets for just an instant before starting down. The most important thing to remember is that the left hip and left side initiate the downswing and the left foot gets firmly planted on the ground before the right half of the body begins to move.

The hitting effort becomes, as shown here, a combination of the pull from the left side and the whipping action of the right forearm.

CRENSHAW:

This is simply the most perfect position one could study.

The hitting effort as shown here becomes a combination of a pull from the left side along with a whipping action of the right forearm.

This position is as true today as it was in Jones's day.

In order to hit the ball solidly, the correct position of the club and arms is from the inside of the ball with the club going out to the target.

This is the total opposite position of the chronic slicer.

People slice because the upper body moves first before the lower body. When the upper body moves, the arms come out and "over" the top of the ball creating an outside-in swing path rather than more properly attacking the ball from the inside out to the target.

Every good player I have ever seen or studied gets in this very position. It's a key to good golf.

■ Long Irons

JONES:

The left leg,
straightening
suddenly at
the knee just
before contact,
produces a
thrust up the
left side
which greatly
increases the
power of the
stroke. To hold
the player
down against
this thrust is
the duty of
the head and
right side
of the body.

CRENSHAW:

You will see many
players today who
appear to have a little
more bow in their
left knee than what
is depicted here.
You'll note that Bob
is using his hands
more in this part of
the swing than Hogan
or Nelson would.

Yesterday players
employed more of a
"hands" swing, while
today we tend to
use the muscles of
the back, shoulders,
hips and trunk.
The modern player
is taught to use
his hands less and
his body more.

CRENSHAW:

No one ever stayed
down and through
the ball better than
Bob Jones.

61

■ Short Irons

JONES:

At address the feet are quite close together to permit easy movement of the hips for this little shot.

CRENSHAW:

Once again, Bob's stance was very narrow.

Even with a shorter swing he still wanted fluidity in his knees and hips in order to get the timing of the stroke. Very clearly he didn't want his upper body isolated just for a short shot. He always thought about a swing and turn.

As elsewhere, the hips and legs begin the backswing, the arms pick up the movement and then…

CRENSHAW:

Bob Jones always felt that more shots were missed in the short range with a stroke that was too abbreviated, rather than one that was too long.

63

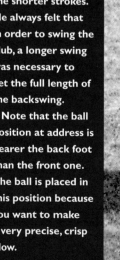

JONES:

…the hands and wrists begin to assist in lifting the club to the top of the swing.

CRENSHAW:

Bob's concept of swinging the clubhead was still very acute even in the shorter strokes. He always felt that in order to swing the club, a longer swing was necessary to get the full length of the backswing.

Note that the ball position at address is nearer the back foot than the front one. The ball is placed in this position because you want to make a very precise, crisp blow.

The thought of hitting a short iron is more of an up-and-down motion. So many people fail to swing the clubhead, especially with a short club.

The key to short iron shots lies in the set-up and how the weight is distributed. Although I use a somewhat wider stance than Bob, my weight is slightly biased to my left side.

JONES:

This is not a full swing, but it is about as far as I like to go with a lofted club for the sake of control.

CRENSHAW:

If you have a short, abbreviated stroke, the tendency is to try to hit the ball rather than swing through it. With a short swing, it becomes a stab or a lunge, with the extra effort trying to move the ball a certain distance.

Bob Jones always laced his writings with an argument for a longer backswing. I also prefer a somewhat longer backswing with my short shots.

JONES:

The start down has been leisurely and the wrist-cock has been preserved almost intact.

CRENSHAW:

Bob Jones made a conscious effort to delay the wrist cock in the forward swing until the very last minute because his swing is a little steeper with a short iron.

CRENSHAW:

In order to put back
spin on the ball,
it's necessary to delay
the wrist cock until
the last minute.
That's as true in Bob
Jones's day as it is now.

JONES:

The stroke is directed slightly downward so that the club rips a divot from the turf after striking the ball.

CRENSHAW:

Again, any good player will try to arrive in this position. He must have the concept of pinching the ball against the turf.

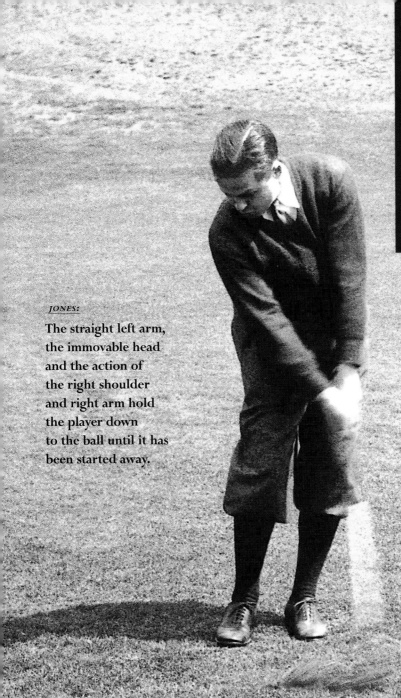

CRENSHAW:

Bob's concept of
the movement and
timing of a swing
is still very valuable
today.
   If your short
game is made up
of short choppy
strokes, concentrate
on swinging the
weight of the club.

JONES:

The straight left arm,
the immovable head
and the action of
the right shoulder
and right arm hold
the player down
to the ball until it has
been started away.

71

■ Short Irons

CRENSHAW:

Perhaps the modern player has a misconception about the use of his full body during a shorter shot. Some teachers may isolate the lower body during the pitching stroke.

JONES:

When the work has been done, the player again relaxes and...

CRENSHAW:

**After all these years,
this is still the most
beautiful finish
position at the end
of a short shot.
It certainly is a good
image to keep in
mind.**

■ Sand Play

JONES:

In playing a full blast or explosive shot from sand, the player faces a little more toward the hole.

CRENSHAW:

There are no appreciable differences between the way Bob Jones played bunker shots and the way we play them today.

74

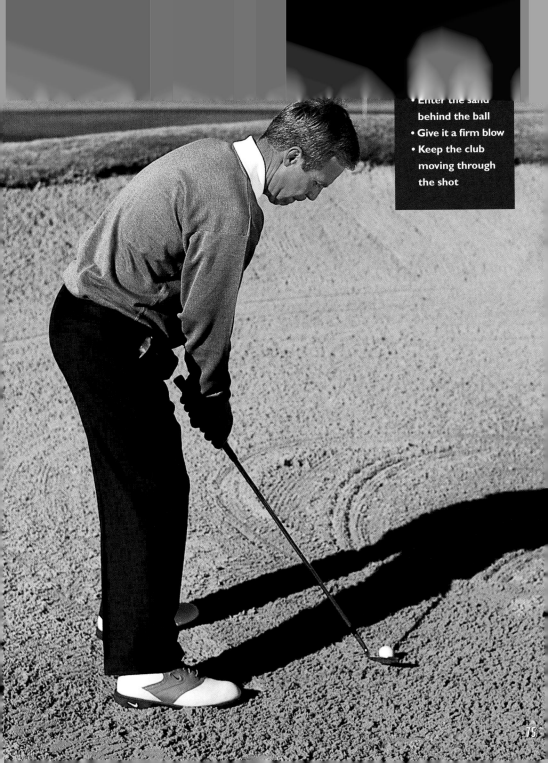

- Enter the sand behind the ball
- Give it a firm blow
- Keep the club moving through the shot

JONES:

The stance is
open with
the right foot
advanced,...

JONES:

...and the face of the club is laid off, so that its effective loft is increased.

CRENSHAW:

The sand shot today has become easier than it was in Jones's time for two reasons. First, the sand we now play out of is more uniform. Second, and more important, the modern sand wedge, with the wide flange on the bottom, literally splashes the ball out of the bunker.

Note the wide flange on the bottom of today's sand wedge in the inset photo.

The same grip as
employed with the
longer clubs is used
for bunker shots.

JONES:

But the grip
is not altered in
any particular
way.

79

JONES:

The backswing is of ample length and more upright than for the ordinary strokes through the green.

■ Sand Play

CRENSHAW:

With a sand shot, if you're having trouble making good contact, try experimenting with the position of the ball in the sand.

JONES:

The clubhead cuts across the line of play from outside to inside, or from right to left,...

82

bunker where it's necessary to stop the ball quickly, I widen my stance and bend my knees more. One of the easiest ways to add height to the shot is to feel like you're sitting down on your right knee at address. You might also wish to choke up a little.

You should feel as if you're "under" the ball more and have a wider base.

JONES:

...and literally blasts
the ball out of the
bunker, along with a
considerable amount
of the sand upon
which it is resting.

CRENSHAW:

The finish of this shot
makes me think the
ball was somewhat
buried. Note that the
position of his hands
and wrists have not
changed appreciably
from the address
position.

When you play a shot out of a buried lie you need to keep your hands moving toward the hole without turning over, just as Bob is demonstrating on the opposite page.

To play this shot, hit down sharply at the edge of the crater formed behind the ball and drive the clubhead down into the sand.

85

CRENSHAW:

One of the most difficult shots in golf is the long bunker shot. The keys to this shot—whether you're in a green-side bunker or a fairway bunker—are to concentrate on your balance and, especially from a fairway bunker, to take enough club.

With long bunker shots, it is important to contact the sand a little closer to the ball. Since these shots are the converse of the short bunker shot, it is also important to stand a little taller to the ball.

JONES:

This is the safest shot to play in order to make certain of getting out of the bunker...

CRENSHAW:

Even though course
maintenance
has improved
dramatically since
Bob Jones's day,
playing a shot from
under a high bank
is still just as difficult.

JONES:

...especially when
the ball is lying
under a high bank.

■ Sand Play

CRENSHAW:

This is more of a shot that you'd play off the fairway when you want to roll it a great distance. Play it off your back foot and give it a firm downward rap on the back of the ball.

JONES:

When the ball is resting on firm sand, and the wall of the bunker is not too high, a clean chip may be attempted.

JONES:

When successful, this little shot is a great stroke-saver, but it involves a deal of risk.

CRENSHAW:

Since it's been more fashionable to play most shots in the air today, rather than on the ground, this type of shot is a fine one to add to your repertoire and use under the right circumstances— whether you're in the bunker or on the fairway.

89

CRENSHAW:

Note how Bob's head is being directed toward the hole as he rotates his body through the shot. It's totally natural.

JONES:

The stroke must be directed downward for if the club strikes the sand before the ball, disaster results, taking first the ball and then the sand,...

JONES:

...for otherwise the
result can be disastrous.

CRENSHAW:

The key here is to play the ball back in your stance and strike the back of the ball first with a sharp descending blow.

■ Putting

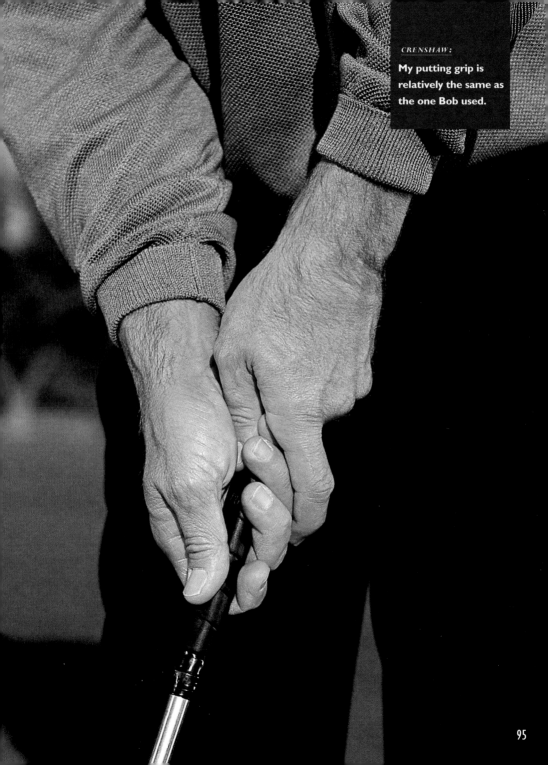

CRENSHAW:

My putting grip is
relatively the same as
the one Bob used.

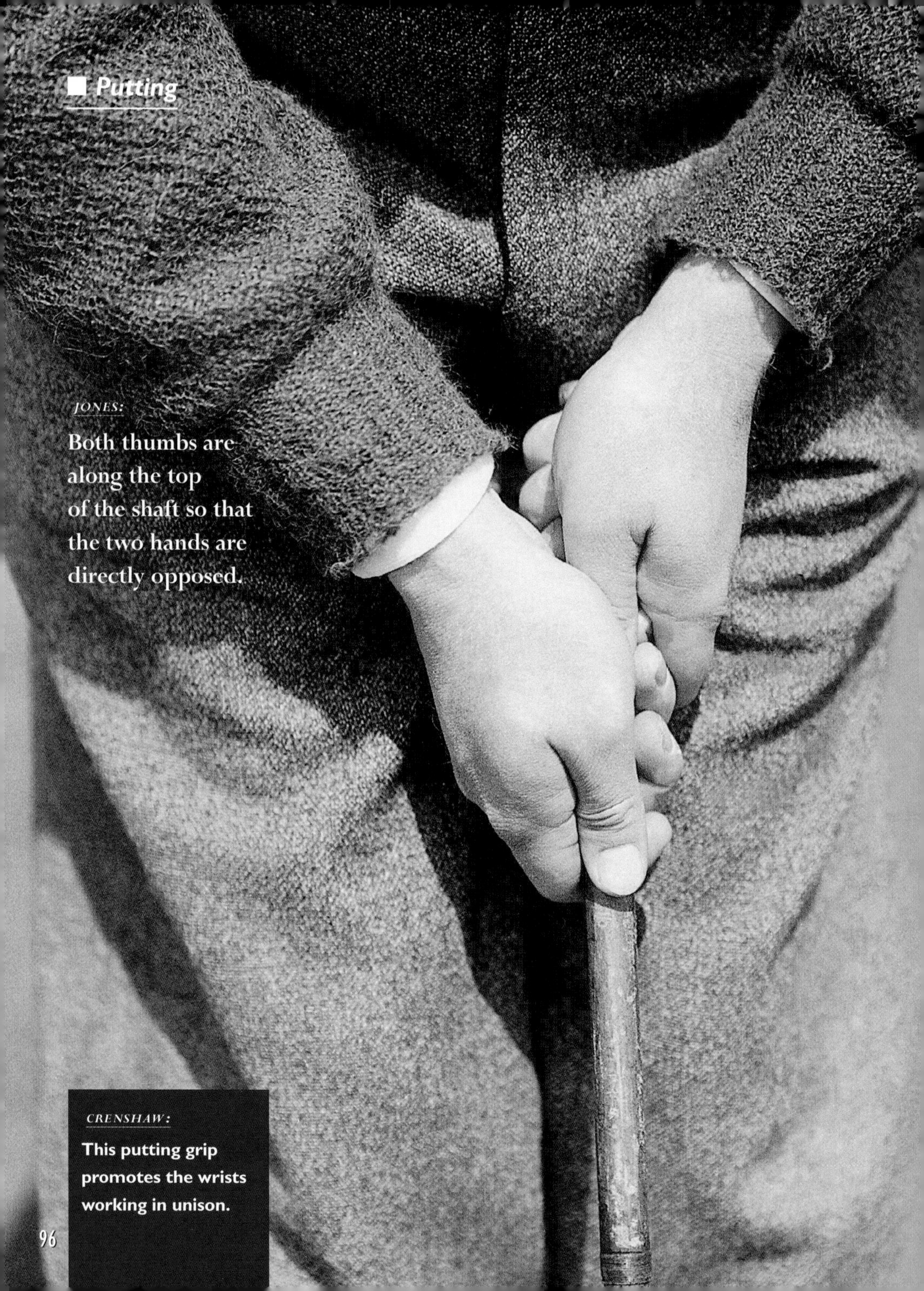

JONES:

**Both thumbs are
along the top
of the shaft so that
the two hands are
directly opposed.**

CRENSHAW:

**This putting grip
promotes the wrists
working in unison.**

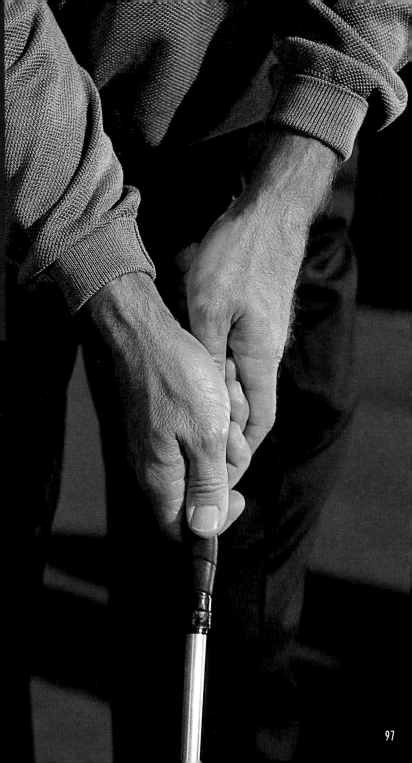

CRENSHAW:

In gripping the putter, I want it to feel as natural as possible.

I have built my putting grip by using the flat top of the putter handle as a guide. As with Bob's grip, I too place my thumbs directly down the shaft.

I start my putting stroke with a little forward press so that my hands are ahead.

■ *Putting*

JONES:

The posture at address is one of comfort and complete relaxation. The knees are slightly bent to avoid any feeling of tension in the player's underpinning.

CRENSHAW:

Interestingly, Bob's putter, Calamity Jane, featured a round grip and was about 34 inches long. It was a light blade with a slight offset. It was one he thought he could *swing* well.

Importantly, Bob's eyes are not directly over the ball—they are slightly *inside* the ball. This position permits freedom in the putting stroke.

I was sixteen.
Although our eyes
are in the same
position relative to
the position of
the ball, my stance is
wider than Bob's.

99

JONES:

The feet are close together and the weight about evenly divided between the two. The left elbow is away from the side so that it can move forward without hindrance.

CRENSHAW:

Today, many believe a prerequisite to good putting is to keep your eyes directly over the ball. Notice that his eyes are lined up *behind* the ball.

Note how close his feet are together. No other great player stood with as narrow a stance as Bob Jones.

Also note that his left arm is bent at the elbow. Consequently, his left shoulder is lower than mine at address.

JONES:

No attempt is made
to "hinge" the stroke
upon either the right or
the left wrist. The arms
and shoulders assist
in the action and the
hips and legs yield
to the movement as the
need arises.

CRENSHAW:

By keeping the left
elbow out from his
body, he wants the
putter face, left hand
and left arm to go
back and toward the
hole. He wanted the
clubface to "float"
through the ball.

JONES:

To step or lock the left wrist
before or as the club strikes
the ball is a serious mistake.
The left arm must move
forward to permit a smooth
completion of the stroke.

JONES:

The backswing brings the club slightly inside the projected line of the putt and the blade is allowed to open naturally.

CRENSHAW:

I couldn't agree more about the path of the backswing; it needs to come slightly inside the line. This is exactly how I feel taking the putter back.

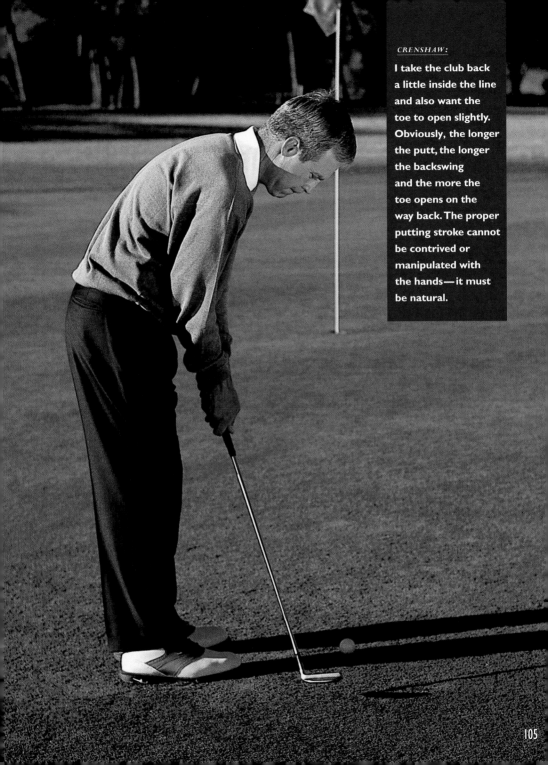

105

JONES:

The club continues its
swing in a flat arc close
to the ground and...

CRENSHAW:

Many instructors now
recommend a static
or rigid position
for the lower body
coupled with a
one-piece movement
of the shoulders
and hands back and
through.

I strongly disagree
with this philosophy
because a rigid lower
body only adds to
tension.

Note how much
Bob's lower body,
particularly his knees
and hips, has moved
from the photo
on page 104 to this
photo and then to the
photo on page 108.

■ Putting

JONES:

…finishes in a sweep that is not restricted by taut muscles.

CRENSHAW:

Note how this is a very smooth, rhythmical sweep. Bob felt that putting was simply the ability to gauge a slope and put the proper pace on the ball.

any rigidity at any point in the putting stroke is the ideal.

As Bob Jones said many times, any stroke in golf must be a swing.

■ Putting

CRENSHAW:

It appears that Bob is playing this little chip with a "chipper" that was made for him to produce run-up shots.

There's no difference in the way Bob is addressing the ball than he does with his putter. However, since the club has a little loft, he's playing it back in his stance.

JONES:

The little chip, from just off the green, becomes in reality a putt...

JONES:

...when played with a special club
of the length and lie of a putter,

CRENSHAW:

Harvey taught us to
play a little 6- or
7-iron from just off
the green to play
this shot. He wanted
us to feel some
movement in our
lower body. He
emphasized that
a putt should feel
the same way.

JONES:

…but with enough loft to pitch the ball onto the closely cut putting surface.

■ *Putting:*

A Comparison

OR	PAR	4	5	4	3	4	3	4	5
4	ELKINGTON	4	5	5	5	5	6	6	6
4	COUPLES	4	4	5	6	6	5	6	6
8	HOCH	8	8	9	8	7	7	7	7
1	CRENSHAW	7	7	7	8	8	8	8	8
1	STRANGE	2	3	4	4	4	5	4	5
7	FROST	7	7	7	7	7	7	7	7
7	MICKELSON	6	5	5	5	4	4	6	
6	HENNINGER	6	6	6	7	7	8	7	8
3	NORMAN	3	4	4	4	4	5	5	6
9	HAAS, J.	9	9	7	6	6	5	5	6

THRU 14

HOCH	7
CRENSHAW	10

■ Putting: A Comparison

Although our putting styles are quite similar, there are several differences. Note how, at address, Bob bends more from the waist, where I prefer to be more erect.

I'm a little open as well but employ a wider stance, with more weight on the left than the right. Note also how Bob is more bent over, with his left arm arched more. Consequently, his left shoulder is lower than mine.

As part of his pre-stroke routine, Bob would place Calamity Jane ahead of his ball and again look at his target. I prefer to leave the putter behind the ball but glance again at the hole and the line once before taking the club back.

If the club is gripped lightly and there is an ample backswing, there is definitelty movement in the lower body. Notice the movement in Bob's knees and hips from the second frame right through the last.

CRENSHAW:

This is a great drill to feel the "swing" of a putt. It's basically the same shot.

■ *Chipping*

JONES:

It is a mistake to try to make one club do for a kinds of chips. Always select a club with whic you can pitch to the ed of the putting surface.

CRENSHAW:

In chipping, it is important to make the club fit the circumstances you're faced with.

Although it looks as if Bob is more right-sided here, he is simply hitting a longer putt. While I definitely feel left-sided when I putt—just as when I chip, Bob seems to be a little more right-sided in his putting.

In the previous frame, it almost looks as if Bob is going to drop the clubhead on the ball, while still keeping the motion smooth. As you can see, he had a little up-and-down movement in his putting stroke.

You clearly get the impression that Bob's putting stroke was a sweep. I try to do the same. The reason that my right arm is straighter than Bob's is that my arms are shorter. Consequently, my stroke is a little bit of a pushing motion.

The most important aspects of good putting are comfort, relaxation and a very light grip. Bob liked to feel that someone could kick the putter out of his hands very easily. I like to feel the same way.

CRENSHAW:

Bob Jones always said never loft the ball unless you absolutely have to. That's still a great piece of advice.

JONES:

Up this close, a number of four or five may be used, and the ball allowed to take its normal roll. The backswing must be of ample length,…

JONES:

...so that the club may be swung through smoothly, without jerk or hurry.

CRENSHAW:

What's important in short shots around the green is the concept of a swing. It's not a stab, it's not a push and it's not a lunge.

CRENSHAW:

In chipping, it's
important to simply
let the club swing
back and through.
That effort alone will
make the ball go.

■ Chipping

CRENSHAW:
There's no better way to express any chip shot than to just get the ball on the green and let it role the intervening way to the hole.

JONES:
Back a bit further, since you still want to pitch to the green without spin if possible, you select a more lofted club, say a number eight,...

JONES:

...and play the
ball precisely the
same way.

CRENSHAW:

There should be
no excessive wrist
action for this stroke.
The simplest, most
straightforward way
to play these shots
is without spin. With
shorter chip shots,
you do this by taking
your wrists out of
the shot. Try not
cocking your wrists.

JONES:

A straightforward pitch, without attempting anything fancy, is always the safest course.

JONES:

There is nothing
fundamental which
distinguishes this
stroke from any
other. The initial
position is entirely
comfortable, the feet
are close together
to make the slight
turn of the hips
a bit easier,…

JONES:

…there is ample use of the hands in the backswing,…

■ **Chipping**

JONES:

…and the crisp,
decisive stroke
at the same
time retains its
smooth, flowing
quality.

CRENSHAW:

I am simply trusting
the loft of the
clubhead in order
to play this shot.
I can't tell you how
many times Harvey
would tell us "you're
not trusting the
manufacturer to get
the job done." In
other words, let the
clubhead do the work
it was designed for.

JONES:

When you get back this far, or have to pitch over a bunker, you choose a niblick, but again, unless the circumstances are extraordinary, you rely upon a normal shot.

133

JONES:

The main thing
is to assure a
complete cocking
of the wrists, a
firm left arm, and
a backswing that
is of ample length.

CRENSHAW:

I think any modern
player would do well
to remember that
the concept behind a
short shot is still a
swing.

JONES:

It is better to have to "float" the club against the ball than to have to make up for a too-short backswing by any extraordinary effort.

135

JONES:

From a lie like this, a short pitch over a bunker provides one of the most difficult problems in the game. You cannot know precisely how much cushioning effect the grass will have.

JONES:

But if you lay back the face of your niblick and loft the ball high in the air you are not likely to go far astray.

This shot is not any
different today,
except that there is
no need to lay back
the face of the club.
Our specialty wedges
today have plenty
of loft to accomplish
this type of shot.
Obviously, this stroke
is as important today
as it was yesterday.

■ *The Stymie*

CRENSHAW:

The stymie, as a specialty shot in match play, was legislated out of existence in 1952 when the USGA permitted marking a ball on the green that interfered with play.

■ The Stymie

CRENSHAW:

Tolley could not negotiate the stymie and Bob won the match 1-up. He was on his way to the most amazing accomplishment in golf history— the Grand Slam!

As a youngster we sometimes played stymies on the practice putting green as a form of competition. It really was a lot of fun. I'd like to see us bring it back for match play competitions.